October 2016

To Bernadette

LADY CASSIE PEREGRINA

Best Wishes

Terry McDonagh

LADY CASSIE PEREGRINA

ARLEN
HOUSE

Lady Cassie Peregrina

is published in 2016 by

ARLEN HOUSE
42 Grange Abbey Road
Baldoyle
Dublin 13
Ireland
Phone/Fax: 353 86 8207617
Email: arlenhouse@gmail.com
arlenhouse.blogspot.com

Distributed internationally by
SYRACUSE UNIVERSITY PRESS
621 Skytop Road, Suite 110
Syracuse, NY 13244–5290
Phone: 315–443–5534/Fax: 315–443–5545
Email: supress@syr.edu

978–1–85132–160–5, paperback

Typesetting by Arlen House

Cover image by Mikyoung Cha

CONTENTS

IV: THE TRAVELLER TAKES HIS HAT *or* WHAT WOULD PEREGRINUS HAVE DONE?

V: I AM CASSIE ON THE CONTINENT

VI: THE FULL CIRCLE – I ALWAYS KNEW I'D HAVE TO TRAVEL, BUT THERE'S AN END TO IT – WELL ISN'T THERE?

INTRODUCTION

It all began in July 2013. Matthew, our son, persisted in his wish to have a dog and, seeing as we were going to be in County Mayo for a year, we were pleased to comply. The Ballyhaunis branch of the ISPCA came up trumps and we met a border collie, Cassie, for the first time. She seemed timid and unsure which would indicate she had not always been well-treated.

We fostered her on a trial basis, but the trial came to an end after about two hours and fostering became permanent. She very quickly got to know the roads, lanes and routines within a radius of seven kilometres of our house in Cill Aodáin, Kiltimagh. We struck up dog-walking friendships and I began taking notes and scribbling a few lines here and there, but it was only when I realised that Cassie must have memories of her own and definite opinions on her current lifestyle, that my scribbling began to shape into poems. Our routine brought me into contact with childhood experiences and memories – people I'd been to school with and grown up alongside. I got closer to the boy hiding within me.

Just after Christmas, the question of *quo vadis* arose and when we decided to return to Hamburg, Cassie's future became an issue. Seeing as we were in this together, provision had to be made for a dog in our Golf Estate. Months passed quickly and when summer came we set out with a carload of belongings and an inexperienced canid. Our journey took us from Cill Aodáin via a ferry from Larne to Cairnryan, to Newcastle by road, to Amsterdam by ferry and, finally, by autobahn to Hamburg where I began the first draft of this poetry collection.

I am indebted to Cassie, family, childhood gallivanting, lifelong friends and experiences, the ongoing struggle with life and mortality, my two sons, Seán and Matthew, granddaughter, Emma, and, especially, to Joanna for her support.

For Joanna and Matthew

Outside of a dog, a book is man's best friend.
Inside of a dog it's too dark to read
– Groucho Marx

LADY CASSIE PEREGRINA

I

I AM CASSIE IN IRELAND

I AM CASSIE

It seems like only yesterday
a dark beast lurked
under my skin, but now
that I've found a family
I don't have to be afraid anymore.
They wait by the gate
looking puzzled when panic
hidden in my bones
twitches like forgotten history.

I am a dog – only a dog – and know
that's what they want me to be.
I don't have to write, juggle words
or read fairytales to young ones.

They're not scared of me – they don't
have to be. I learned not to bark
in my previous home where I was
beaten for being a dog and dumped.
Sometimes when I wake in a mess of sweat,
I imagine I have another name – not Cassie.
I try not to peep over my shoulder into the past.

MORNINGS

Mornings about eleven we go walking,
languishing along lanes
saturated in marvels – mainly,
but it can be testing when
walkers wallow in wind-chill-chat,
sources of sciatica or central heating oil.

I try never to grumble, be contrary
or get above my station. Maybe
that's just me but, by the same token,
dreaming of rounding up sheep
is one thing.
Singing for supper – that's another.

During these challenging gossip-stops
I duck and secrete in the long grass
to avoid clashes with canine cousin and kin
who seem to know little of phantom fears.

It makes me sick having to listen
to fellow dogs rabbiting on
about table-leg pickings and crumbs
as their keepers pamper in tea and plenty.

Given all that, in a far distance
I still hear, taste and shrink
from the malice of gore
no creature should have to endure.

These days I indulge in the sound
of food on my plate – in
the flavour and twinkle of candles –
as I ride out to sleep.

I have a blanket
in one corner and a rug in another
where I can sink into miles of dog saga.

My head is up and trained on the horizon.
The past with its clanking chains is past.

BACKBONE

Last autumn while burrowing
for dog spirits in waste ground,
I stumbled on a string
of human vertebrae
that didn't constitute a backbone.

They must have belonged
to my previous owner.

RABBITS

When I open an eye
to watch a pair of baby rabbits
nibbling at dandelion sprouts
in the front garden,
my single wish is
to snap this picture and frame it.

NOTHING IS AS IT SEEMS

I'm only a dog but I see what I see
and hear what I hear
from my very own space
under stars, tables or starters orders.
I do try to be in tune
with the chimes of our planet.

I could be losing compassion
but some adults roll out
such bizarre rhetoric
they seem to be out of touch.
Lose me, they do – going on
about education and politics
in that relentless, encore way
when their pool of arty banter
deserts them
– when silence seems unbearable.

I see children and teachers
trundle off each morning
like swarms of bees
heading for artful pollen fields.

Noble thoughts about school
often seem out of bounds – a bit
like a love-affair with a mink coat,
being happy in hospital
or exposing your fantasies in church.

I'm jealous: my hope of dog-school
seems slim
– I'm more dog
at back door type
or dog in photo
unless, of course, a thoughtful pupil

smuggles me in or a sensitive teacher
appreciates the role of a border collie
when skirmishes are about to blow up.

I was rescued by the ISPCA – caring people.
I got fed, could stretch my legs and learn
to open my arms to welcome a new family.

At times, when contemplating my past,
I vanish into a grey cloud,
rattle like a poltergeist
or rip at beech-tree-bark and howl.

I often lie there thinking
nothing is as it seems.

Even if I can't read or write
I can imagine sun flooding a page,
an armchair out on high waves,
a mouse whistling in an attic
or I can tune in to the true note
in a creature heart.

POINT OF VIEW

Cosy *stuff* can be a bit excessive:
over here on the Foxford blankie, Cassie.
over here on the granny rug, Cassie.

And if I get wet – which is natural in rain,
they even resort to drying my paws.
You'd imagine a drop of rain was smelly.

All I want to do is to go speedo
about the house
to really amuse myself
but I don't because they are ok.
Though I really enjoy pure wet.

I often give them that doggy look,
lackadaisical like,
casually offering a submissive paw.
It works: *Good Cassie! Is Cassie fed?*

It's organic for me. I wish I could tell
oaf-dog-down-the-way
of my tasty morsels jangling
like new coins in my dish.

I'm a quick learner. I don't bark much
and I've no intention of running away.
It's because she's a Collie.
They're so intelligent.
Thanks people. Couldn't agree more.
Must keep that in mind.

Between ourselves, a friend's dog
is a terrier type – all bark and snarl.
I'd prefer a path without pity to his camaraderie
– any day!

EMBARRASSING HABITS

You'd sometimes see me crouching
when I sense another beast – nothing
special – just the working dog in me
wanting to work. But when I catch myself
cowering like a thief behind a hedge,
I quickly straighten up – pretending
to look this way and that – covering up

as if looking for the gateway to another world
as if being a bit embarrassed mattered
as if about to burst into song with cows looking on.

A Dog's Life – According to Cassie

I've got eyes, and when I look at people in heels,
no heels, two legs and artificial faces,
I am happy with my bowl of food and water.

I cannot articulate, write or use a mobile,
thank doG
though I'm able to leather out vigorous yelps
when jig-acting or buck-leping at the seashore.

Beware of the hedonist in me
that knows how to indulge
in the glow of honeysuckle
and in mouthfuls of turf magic
on my silken frolics along bog roads.

I feel lucky that I have the sun, moon
and raindrops as constant companions.

When reaching for the stars, I lie
on my back and poke four legs in the air.

TIME OUT

I'm not a great one for barking or noise.
Forgive me if I've said that already.
What I like most is dossing about
after I'm done with breakfast,
my walk and usual doggy functions.

Neither am I a composer
with a mind full of top notes
and high stepping – more
a herding dog that doesn't herd.

I saunter, engrossed in shades of sheep
on a faraway hill, contemplating
bunches of birds trucking with berries.

I'm not even a philosopher – just a dog
rambling about – hating cats, counting
the hours up and down, back to
the last dinner and forward to the next.

On the Subject of Cows

It doesn't take much to throw cows
completely out of thwack.

It's so easy it's hardly worth the effort.
No fun. They're dense.

I stroll into the field where
they are chomping – noisy as ever.
All I have to do is sidle up to
the whole herd of them
and bingo, they stop munching.

Mesmerised, they lump together
gaping at me in a way
only cows can gawp, as if
their field was threatened
or bulls-eyes were being
lobbed at them
from the other side of the hedge.

There's nothing more to be said
on the subject of cows – for now.

A Dog Speaks on a Derelict Graveyard and Death

When people speak about Killedan House tradition
they often mention the dogs' graveyard as if
it was animate and just under the skin of house rhetoric.

Graveyards are soundless and speechless. As soon as
a wet sod puts the lid on a beast's life, the most rabid
are mute – no more barking up the wrong tree.

In quiet moments I see the reptile tongue of death
tidying up the unviable – ruthless as a cold slab of winter
making way for the fresh yelp of first daffodils.

Even in absolute shambles, a dog's gravestone
would be a rare museum feature – an artefact
on display or a sculpture that will outlive me.

I lie here on the doorstep imagining canine spirits
between airstream and slipstream – seeing them
soar and funnel their way to nameless worlds,

but a dead dog is dead, cold as handlebars in frost,
colourless as white,
silent as an alpine cow without a bell.

Images of jumbled bones and sprawling roots
in the derelict dogs' graveyard leave me cold
but when my end does come, I'd be proud

to be borne there
draped in the colours of my breed.

THE CAR

Silly prattle, a dog doesn't understand, is bad enough
but to be shoehorned into a shifty-looking car
with no idea where it could lead to, can be daunting.

However, I have to admit that apart from
a scary trip to the vet
involving a jab and an embarrassing trim,

I'm full of it when we embark on bubbly trips
to places that are more like neglected jumpers
and banana skins than scenic experiences

and I'm okay when they set off on their mystery tours
without me, but I almost purr – not quite – when
the engine drones back up the road into my cycle of life.

No Comment

it's a dog's life
top dog
every dog has his day
a dog without a tail has a weekend
tail wagging the dog
dog into them lads
black dog
I've been dogged by bad luck
a dog's dinner
sick as a dog
call off your dogs
in the doghouse
a dirty dog
the hair of the dog
raining cats and dogs
let sleeping dogs lie
you lucky dog
haven't a dog's chance in hell
meaner than a junkyard dog
there's life in the auld dog yet
can't teach an old dog new tricks
hot dog
dog eat dog.

II

ROUND IN CIRCLES WITH CASSIE

SETTING OUT IN 2014

It's March. After breakfast, I jump on my bike
when it's my turn to do my dutiful round
with Cassie, our border collie. It's as if time
opens curtains to underwrite a spring landscape.

Last year we didn't have a dog – didn't
really want one – but now we do:
a high priestess in black and white who
is teaching me to snarl into snapping elements.

I don't blame the rain. These days there are
new sounds in hedgerows where nothing
but thorn or thistle used to touch me – and
roads went nowhere, except to Kiltimagh

or other places with friendlier climates. The first
hundred metres of my seven kilometre trip
is hemmed in by a pair of tattered fences
down to the bend – *the corner* we called it.

As a child these fences kept my ball on track
for hours on end or it was a stockpile
of glowing blackberries for jam
in the best and most wholesome of times.

When visitors came we were keen to show off
the High Fort – *Lios Árd* – write our names
into ancient woodlands, mimic teachers and
be proud to tell tales of the blind poet, Raifteirí.

Round *the corner* down on the left, there's
no trace of a sad thatched cottage that sat
huddled and perfect against a tragic story
of a broken family and a man who took his life.

The lane is potholed. Last year I cycled paths
smooth as a map of Europe in Hamburg. I was
at home then and I'm at home now. Cassie and I
gimmick and bump down to the end of the *boreen*.

We turn right up a little slope and face the bog road
lined with feral scrub and wayward wood, layered
with good and bad memories – decades of delight.
Dread was bottled up between here and Canavan's Cross.

At the Iron Gate – the back entrance – I look up
to the lean beech trees crowning the Hight Fort
– a home to witchcraft-and-legend-scrubbed-clean
by church, school machinery and sanitised kitchens.

The Well Under the Fort

There are no ripples in a well, but there were
sounds in the one I have in mind.
It was a childhood grotto in a whitewashed frame

with slab steps
leading down
to dark boggy water
too magical to sprinkle.

The Virgin Mary and witches would have
spent time here.
Solace and comfort was to be had
on dour days
and silence was not divided by time.

Fairies came, drank, left traces along the wind,
trails to black and white thorn up to the tip
of the High Fort or down to my heathen graveyard.

The well was
a right of way
to a right of passage.

RESUMING

Cassie trots alongside my bike in a mixture
of black, white and a roll or two of fat
that suggests there's more to her than just
the border collie she would have us believe.

We meet a Nissan just before the next bend,
pull over in tandem to avoid pitfalls – we
progress like a practised couple fixated on
the dangers of late frolics or last winter's frost.

Still in Cill Aodáin, on down past a few houses
smiling like winking window boxes against
a backdrop of fading years and memories
of the Pollagh River as full of fish as an exile's dream.

CILL AODÁIN GRAVEYARD ON THE POLLAGH RIVER

Cill Aodáin graveyard is back on its feet:
headstones are standing better than ever,
bits of history are tacked on to walls;
not enough for a talkative village, but
enough for now – it's a clean monument.

It pulls in the sun, but it has lost its flair for weeds
and our hunt for relatives under growth.
My great grandfather's stone is plain to be seen –
his memory needs a touch up.

This used to be an important place.
I had monks from my father,
fairy funerals from a neighbour
and jackdaws for fear.

I heard a fiddler from far away
and we saw ordinary young fishermen
swap lean worms on a Sunday.

There's open air mass
once a year.

The pattern has darkened: eels and moorhens
have lost out to a drainage scheme.
The hundred yards down
to the meeting of the Pollagh and the Glore,
before they went on to India,
used to be forbidding and swampy
– *would you believe it!*
and a big horse cleared a fence,
never to be seen again
– *it's owner had tinkered with blackthorn,*
said a child, from a fairy tree.

The soft elements
have become sullied and foul.
We lit bonfires
on St John's Night!

Once when I was fishing, a king sailed past.
I was busy with the one that got away, so
I only nodded. The king called on me to follow.

I knew I would when elsewhere spoke up.

RESUMING

There is something about the Pollagh bridge:
you lean over the parapet, focus on the current
and are cascaded off to destiny in metaphor.
The places I went to helped to cut me loose.

Water on the brain and a bridge too far – it's time
to face into the mist and south west breeze; time
to remember wading the river when I was
as much out of my depth as Persephone in winter.

We're still on track. Now in foreign Pollronaghan
between the bridge and the defunct railway tracks
and over the tracks, past industry and cosy houses,
to the Glore River where spawning salmon were poached.

The railway crossing
once a gateway to somewhere
now leading nowhere.

On the other side of Cill Aodáin Graveyard, the Pollagh
and Glore meet to form the Gweestion. The space
between them may not be as rich in history
as the pocket between the Tigris and the Euphrates

but here are fields with words waiting to be tilled.
We're on a slope upwards. The further I get from home
the closer I get to it. Here is the womb that bore me
and might be the tomb I will return to. Why do I say this?

Now really foreign: about two kilometres from source.
A left swing at the top of the slope into Treankeel
with a good breeze to egg us on – between my lines,
strings of a fiddle, between gods – poetry does this.

No wild oats left or right. It's spring. Some wild oats
were sown in houses and hidden in confessional boxes,
but reward was reaped elsewhere in colourless crowds
or draughty streets, beyond the echo and scent of gold.

To Cassie

If I could see through your dog eye, would your
canine spirit allow me insight into thoughts
and dreams that men, ripping from forests and fields,
share with their gods in a pay-as-you-go age.

To be what I'm unable to be, I'd love to be a
dog – a trained beast: *where did you get him?*
I'd like to know if dogs mock when they obey
or raise a doggy paw in that pleading sort of way.

RESUMING

This is a lovely stretch with the breeze at my back,
all in baffled quiet until a boy racer blazes past
making a fuss with gloves on. Clouds disperse and
gather in the restless breeze like coins and lotto tickets.

Next left and down the slope across the stream into
the townland of Treenfounghnane with the cleanliness
of the morning full in my face – through our second
railway crossing – the same neglected tracks we crossed

further back. The gates have rotted without trace and
the gatehouse crumbled. A big family lived here. I went
to school with some of them in Lismirrane, but when
I try to haul in names and faces, I only see silhouettes.

parallel iron tracks
rusting records and memoirs
of opaque childhood

From the top of Treenfounghnane hill I look
left to the distant High Fort – faintly right
to my old school as old cold death applauds.
A landscape holds secrets and shields for the heart.

Onwards faithful collie – between here and
Cloghar bridge there are dogfights to be avoided.
I still see fishermen in waders Sunday after Sunday.
We fished with worms and sometimes jumped in.

There's silence on the tender slice of road
as I turn left into Cill Aodáin again. Stop!
Next right, my old school, now an Arts Centre.
My mother taught here – her songs cling and linger.

We'd grieve as one Principal beat cold into
warm mornings and killed speech in its prime.
I grit my teeth and move faster. Perhaps
the dead can atone for the pain they inflicted. Amen.

Now back in my childhood heartland
– a landscape unreal, divine and articulate.
I realise love is unearthly and not tied to place
but place is place and place is homeland.

My true home is always shifting but remains intact.
It's deeply imbedded in my passage from
first to last light. My address is a quiet place
with a bunch of words and ones who understand.

III

CASSIE ON HEADING FOR THE MAINLAND OF EUROPE

DARK DAYS

I am a proud collie. I realise
I have to go out into the world,
wag my tail and
be a good-natured sheepdog,
yet there are times when
my tail just won't budge,
phases when I wake to dark noises
reminding me of sombre thuds
in the dank air – when not even
counting sheep on back hills
nor sunlight whispering solace
in the green garden
can keep me this side of the edge.

It was clear something was afoot.
It felt like flat and lifeless,
like a time to run inside and hide.

QUO VADIS AND DOUBT

The wheels were pumped.
The whole idea of taking off
on a long trip made me feel
a stomach-ache coming on.
I wondered if their blindness
was obvious to them.

I felt pulled too far away from myself
so I chose the doorstep
where the sun could wrap itself around my world.

For the trip, I'd got a special drinking dish
that wouldn't splash – which was useful
on bumpy bits when lost in this or that dream.

I've always tried to take refuge in dog-song,
in the reverie of river sound memories,
in walks along lanes as evenings stretched
like welcome mats on the far horizon.

And then there are the everyday complexes:
could I have badger traits
or be a fox in disguise – subject change please.

I recall a dog stop in a strange place.
On with my lead of course – they
didn't know I wouldn't run away –
then off again into more futility
– who was I to complain – it was more
about them than me – I'm only a dog.

SETTING OUT IN THE REAL PRESENT

The car was packed with a grid
between me and the back seat
to keep me in my place it would seem.

I gather we are insured down to the spleen
lest we mislay common sense, *so*
we've no worries to worry about.
I've been spayed, had no rendezvous
and have my toilet habits under control.

There's a notion that I could be a problem
in the first four hours – *not on your bone.*

I'll slip into my halo, increase volume on
quality days and put my head into sleep mode.

Once I almost put a tomcat out
of one of his miserable lives.
I'll have that sweet memory
between here and Larne.
I feel better today for some reason.

TO THE FIRST FERRY

Job done. They looked as relaxed as free-range chickens
when we arrived at the ferry at Larne. It's the moment,
but mostly the memory that makes things real, I suppose.

The boat refused to be still – seemed to defy the laws of nature
while I sat it out like a bulging crop in waiting.
There was nothing to draw me in or push me out. It just was.

We docked to winching, banging and clanging at Cairnryan.
It was raining into the soft Scottish afternoon as our car
balanced and swayed like driftwood sniffing a new shore.

I realize I'm talking like a human – I'm
not making it up – I'm regurgitating, but
how else can I convey my experiences to you.

Read on.

I'm a foreign dog in a foreign country, straying
even further away from the turf smells
I'd grown accustomed to – from the lanes
that stretched out like friendly snakes and ladders.

DREAM ON

A wolf came to me in a dream the other night,
not as a wolf from now
but as a wolf a thousand years from now.

It looked blameless and incorruptible
almost gullible by a living room fire
as if not conscious of its savage history.

What if I came to a wolf in its dream one night
not as a dog from now
but as a dog a thousand years from now,

would my way of looking all dandy and dapper,
dancing about on two or three legs,
imply I'd once been a loyal four-footed friend?

ABROAD

I had my first walk on foreign soil
in the grounds of a big hotel in Scotland.
With the bedroom floor to myself
I felt like a dried out tongue panting.
So far – so good.
That old chestnut!
but I've got a mouth
to tell myself
this is far from good.

IV

THE TRAVELLER TAKES HIS HAT
or
WHAT WOULD PEREGRINUS HAVE DONE?

LEAVETAKING

Man – barely out of its antediluvian habitat
mooching in twilight zones
between inner and outer worlds
between left and right brain
between despair and hope – must journey.

The traveller takes his hat,
looks about
and says goodbye
to the last part of his past tense.

The journey from Mayo to Hamburg
through doors, bread rolls, channels
nodding in and out of words for
dawn
daylight
twilight
darkness
with a dog in the back
that can't spell,
can't know what's to come.

ROUTINE

Relaxed get up wash dress breakfast scratch brush teeth
Onwards check self in mirror check hair in shop window
Uptown pretend to work display anger lust yearn despair
Tired have lunch hurry up smile laugh have a pint at break
Imbibe struggle all afternoon leave the job do other things
Nervous fingers along railings run same fingers through hair
Exhausted hide feelings home change to casuals nap telly sleep.

AND MORNINGS ALONE

With the strange religion of nature in my ear
I walk down to a riverbank
hearing the voice of a lost child
from the far west on the breeze
singing in vanishing languages.

Just round the corner
a rejected woman chants
in mysteries
to the relics of her ancients,

to the children of a foreign family
trying to become less foreign,
trying to change colour,
trying to become people they can't.

I step out into another day.
I have no other choice.

A Mirror to Self

This is a journey from dawn to dark.
When the sun no longer rises
and I lie in unrelenting darkness,
will I have come to my final end?

We've been in Ireland for a year.
In that time we've acquired
a dog – a true friend.
Cassie,
should we go or should we stay?

Progress is an uneasy companion.
With Cassie in the back
and our son, Matthew, on the back seat,
we point our heads round and hard
towards the goal ahead, hiding
the flood and ebb between heart and eye.

As they go through the valley of the weeper
they make it a place of springs – Psalm 84.

Dawn in Cill Aodáin – morning in
Sligo, Leitrim, Cavan, the Border,
Belfast, Larne and the boat at noon
in Dumfries and Galloway
to Castle Douglas
to fix a foundation in darkness.

Do we prefer our own countryside
or
do we live at the mercy of the wind?

Peregrinus had wanted to put a tip of gold
on a golden life. I'd love be a cynic

but I see myself pulling the motor
that's meant to push me. It's all uphill.

My tongue is floundering
out of its depth in pools of doubt
heading for Newcastle
with the road shortening – the end
of a legend or perhaps the beginning.

SAILING

Sailing lightward and sailing darkward
is a hard sailing
even in a car
between couplets
going nowhere in particular.

RAIN

How pleasant it is to step out of the car
into Scotch mist close to Hadrian's Wall.
Overhead a shape like a fisher boy
seems to cast hooks into tons of drizzle,
snatching at wayward sunbeams
through gaps in breaking cloud.

He glances this way and that – furtive
over one shoulder, then the other,
hungry for features in elusive clouds,
for pieces of golden light,
for a last line to give his poem an end.

His rod swings like a great pendulum,
like an impatient pen hovering
above a page that won't be pushed
into accepting just any word thrown at it.

The pen flits and snaps.
The page stays blank.
The cloud doesn't break.
The sun won't be drawn.

In despair, the boy grabs his kit,
taking wing in a whirl of importance
like a teenager with something to do.

What I'm talking about here is rain
– lots of it. It falls on

bishops
cynics
dumps
eavesdroppers
frogs

glaciers
hogs
iguanas
jockeys
kangaroos
lads
mums
nuns
orphans
pigs
rats
Sabbath
temples
us
vicars
worms
Xmas
yabbos
zealots

and
seeing as we're all going
to hell – hopefully
a downpour will come to our rescue.

It's time to return to the car.
I'm dampish and Cassie
will be humming in her own way.

When I look up at night
I'm sometimes greeted
by a huge moonlit smirk.

JOURNEYING CAN BE

as endless as the mystery
of the Mona Lisa,

as complete as leaves
creating shapes in autumn,

as satisfying as a well-worn book
by an open window,

as perfect as echolocation
in a busy orchard,

as uncertain as a paper airplane
in a hurricane,

as illusory as a replica of now
round the next bend.

NEWCASTLE

We didn't have a navigation system
but we wormed our way through
to Newcastle's Port of Tyne with
me drumming fingers on the steering
under the steady influence of a route planner.

This shopping centre at the port
is no pristine *Tir na nÓg* – it's
a life before death and no more.
We found a disused bus park
and pretended to look the other way
as Cassie did what dogs do next to a daisy.
Then silent as a church collection,
she jumped into the car while we
hit for the shops like a trio of scallywags.
With my wallet on my shoulder
sure no one can be bolder, thought I
with an eye on a reduced hardback jotter
for the best of poetry yet to come.
I put reserve on hold and splashed out a fiver.
Joanna hit upon an offer on a mislaid item.
Matthew unearthed an inflatable computer game.

We floated about like souls on aerial display.
I considered stoning myself to kill time, but
seeing as I was closer to death than birth,
I thought I'd leave it to natural causes.
Instead, I examined myself for traces of youth
in a Subway window.
A head waiter spotted me and invited us in.
It was Subway all the way
through chip and chin till our boat came in.

To Amsterdam

On to the ferry
all at sea and owning up to being human,
whispering out, *poetry is a mug's game*
but obviously not loud enough
or was I keeping it to myself
in case security men in plain clothes
picked up on my dream
of reciting a stint of fresh doggerel
for your pleasure
from the corner of the lounge bar?

It was early evening. We were
heading east – not quite the Orient
but to where cross-dressing
is not just a rugby player's prerogative.
Cassie was in her cave.
The deck bar was filling up with ring-leaders
in stag and hen-party attire. Mothers-in-law
looked the other way worrying about welfare.
Couple rituals were as coy as could be.

The place was askew with high-five joviality.
Go to your berth if you want to be lonely.
This is not a mollycoddling studio, was the motto.
It was happiness all the way or nothing.
Some sat with legs under them paying attention
to their own faces and those of others.

As the evening progressed, mouths changed shape
and laughter took on a different tone.
The restaurants filled up with all-in meals.
A singer sang of a mother he'd once loved.
Deck was waiting for me to chant
to the setting sun – I declined, imagining

an Albatross on all fours
coming at me out of the mist. We left the bar
and slept as soundly as pre-programmed tablets.

THE ROAD TO HAMBURG

In the car with two ferry crossings behind us
and an open road up ahead – it's hot.

We've only got the rhythm of hearts,
the radio and each other for company.

The rear mirror is my constant companion
but no matter how often I check, our home

in the west of Ireland draws further away.
The autobahn is noisy – the price of place.

Quiet is a matter of the head. We follow signs
that seem wrong at the time
but which turn out right – numbered roads
sort themselves. There is no turning back.
We'll stop near the border
Enschede?
Right
Need a break.

We do and watch the heat blister
sallow, insipid strings of fervour
from earth to sky.
I wish it would melt and have done with it.

We are on the road again longing for a return
to the sweet juice of Mayo mist – even to

the tugging of downpours and wind. We've
been away for a year – now returning

to the familiar, unfamiliar chatter of markets,
late night normality and early morning duty.

This is real. Three hours from now, we'll
be sitting in a café in Hamburg surrounded

by city décor hurrying past. We know it well.
We've got no ancestors but we do have haunts.

Sometimes the adopted seems almost as strange
as an exhibition of ancient cave etchings.

There will be different words for things that
mean the same in any language – differences

are chiselled in history. It is their sweet sounds
that keeps us coming and going. Fear of dogs

and insects remain fears of dogs and insects – for
some believers dogs must return again and again

to be purified. I don't expect to see Cassie twice.
The ghost imprint of having two homes is lifting.

We drink from chalices. We have homes
by sacred rivers. We have buried fears

by the Elbe and the Pollagh. Occasionally,
we trust ourselves to dig them up.

This is one of these times. Hamburg is there
in front of us, large as life – let us embrace.

V

I am Cassie on the Continent

THE ROAD TO HAMBURG

In the car with two ferry crossings behind us
and an open road up ahead – it's hot.

We've only got the rhythm of hearts,
radio and each other for company.

We know how to keep that dingo lingo
for shoreline friends or for the back hills.

There I am – at it again – daydreaming
with cars whizzing like piano scales

and me as well cushioned as any old rug
in my space on the autobahn to Hamburg.

It's hot but we've got air conditioning
and I'm reasonably well combed.

There goes that radio again.
If you want to get to know the worst in me,
turn that radio up. Talk later.

A dog whimpers, dreams and breathes
in its sleep, I'm told.

Picnic Times

I am a dog
on a speckled blanket
in a Golf Estate
in scorching sun
an outcast
sniffing for approval
waiting for orders
from three humans
who'd be lost
without maps
but these humans
didn't need direction
when we walked
hand-in-hand
on our honeymoon
picnic days
without end
without a lead
without need of lead
under full, crescent
or half moons
along lanes
where I'd curl up
and do nothing
but admire
baby rabbits
learning their trade
figures in fields
and I would chuckle
cause I didn't have
to defend or defy.

Compared to this
those were picnic times.

I've defended the homeland
for long enough.
Let's see what lies ahead.

HAMBURG

Now in Hamburg I think in echoes.
I tell my tale as if it were real.
I used to be in a chapter of ample
and innocence. In the city
I'm in a haze of feet and signposts.

Night and day career past and I ask:
is this the start of sadness – I'm
amazed at how dogs grin and stare.

I wonder when I can stop
being scared on streets
where almost anything
can crop up. To be continued.

I WON'T STEP OFF THE KERB

City people are kind
but they take the music out
of a dog's step
the moment the lead is introduced.

I'm not a fool. I'd never try to escape.
I have memories of scuttling and loping
next to the rear wheel of a bicycle,
within earshot of giggling frogs,
cranky hedgehogs and wild woodbine.

Without a care in the world
we'd stop
to let cars pass.

If you could see into my head,
you'd see a dog born to be free
and fed. Don't lecture me.

I'm just a bundle of black and white
with feet of chimes and a herding instinct.
Release me from my lead
and I promise I won't step off the kerb.

VI

THE FULL CIRCLE
I ALWAYS KNEW I'D HAVE TO TRAVEL
THERE'S AN END TO IT ... WELL, ISN'T THERE?

ABOUT LASSIE AND CASSIE

When I was a lad I knew all about
the adventures of Lassie. I wanted
to be Jeff or Timmie – just a
mischievous boy with his own collie.

Some friends had dogs but Lassie,
our favourite, was in storybooks
and comics.
Our Cassie is real –
about thirty-five in human years and
I confess to being a cacophony of dog years
clinging to loose ends.
I wonder if she sees the new moon?
Enough!
I'm barking up the wrong tree.
It's not about me.
Cassie is the story
and the story is about Cassie.

THE FULL CIRCLE

And it's about travelling, isn't it?
There are those who shake their
heads and fists at Picasso
while digging their own grave.
They plant skid marks next to an outer wall
to mark their territory
and hang ancestral photos along hedgerows
as proof of their indestructibility.

The birds of the air shake their heads
and listen to the caged screams
of a father – jaded by the flight of money
or a mother – black around the eyes
from pinning her kids to concrete mixers.
She has tales of gods to fasten them
to fear of hell.
In dreams
she knows there are galaxies
but she dare not look up in case
she sees her offspring dissipating into crowds.

Perhaps I am the one limping in litanies
behind my father
on our way home from the marketplace.

We were at the circus
and it was very good
We were at the dance
and it was very good
We were in the church
and it was very good
We were in the bank
and it was very good
We were at school
and it was very good

We built a house
and it was our saviour
We ignored daft people
and it was very good
We knocked the nonsense out of children
and it was very good
We repaired the roof
and it was very good
We christened our children chaste
and it was very good
We lived a life of fear
and it was very good
We instilled guilt into our family
and it was very good.

We've never moved and thanked God for that.
Oh, my God!

I am drinking coffee in *Die Kleine Konditorei*
in Osterstrasse Hamburg
wondering how this journey began and how
it might have been otherwise.
The *Hamburger Sparkasse* on the corner
looks after my money.
I have a roof over my head.
I have a family and some guilt
to my name. Secretly I don't like graffiti
unless it's to my taste, of course.
It's wet outside and not everyone is dressed
to my liking.

Recently I've begun dreaming
in German

about a journey around a galaxy
in a full circle
from the west of Ireland
to Hamburg
and
from Hamburg
to the west of Ireland
and I can't get off.

There are deep valleys,
light, dark and a wet sun
smiling at a lake
where spirits seem to congregate.

I cannot see clearly into the lake
and no matter how hard I look
my own reflection just won't come up.

You'd wonder about water, but
there are things to be done:
Cassie needs a walk and a morsel
and Matthew finishes school in a few hours.

I always knew I'd have to travel
but there's an end to it … *well, isn't there?*

But no, there probably isn't. It's spirit
to flesh to earth to bone.

Now months into eating hot and cold.
A neighbour has passed away
and we cluster in our block
like a clan huddling around last words.

This morning, on foot, I circled the Alster
with a friend – marvelling at water –
wondering if home was a matter of the heart
in a no man's land of weeping or
not weeping in everyman's land of spring.

The full circle won't fill in. We don't own
the intense and softer laughter of the wind
and even when I look harder I cannot fathom
the silence between horizon and horizon.

Cassie is sleeping – quiet as incense – like
a dreaming harp string in a timeless ritual.
Uplands call – flat lands call – somewhere
a cord is struck in a symphony to new season.

Acknowledgements

To Brian Mooney and IRD Kiltimagh for placing my poem, 'The Last Bard', on display in the market square.

Thanks to the members of Authorenvereinigung Hamburg (Writers Union Hamburg) as well as Verband Deutcher Schriftsteller – V.S. Hamburg (Association of German writers, Hamburg).

Thanks are due to the following journals, anthologies, radio, TV and web outlets where some of my work has been published or aired at different times: *Poetry Ireland Review*; *Cyphers*; *The SHOp*; *Live Encounters* magazine; *Weinachtsgeschichten am Kamin,* Hamburg; *The Stinging Fly*; Hamburger Abendblatt; *Cúirt Journal*; *Stony Thursday Book*; *The Caterpillar*; *Prairie Schooner*; *Connacht Telegraph*; *Galway Advertiser*; *Agenda Poetry,* London; Claremorris Community Radio; *The Western People*; Midwest Radio; *Mayo News*; *Southword*; Westport Community Radio; *Tintean,* Melbourne; New*leaf* Bremen; *Crab Orchard Review*; Kieler Nachrichten Germany; Hamburger Ziegel; Hamburg 1 TV; *Present Tense, Words & Pictures,* Co Mayo.

Terry McDonagh, from Cill Aodáin, Kiltimagh, lives in Mayo and in Germany. His poetry collections include: *The Road Out, A World Without Stone, Boxes, A Song for Joanna, Cill Aodáin and Nowhere Else, In the Light of Bridges – Hamburg Fragments, The Truth in Mustard, Ripple Effect, Echolocation.*

Terry has taught English at the University of Hamburg and was Drama Director at the International School Hamburg.

His poem, 'Out of the Dying Pan into the Pyre', was longlisted for The Poetry Society poetry prize 2015 and 'From a Hauptbahnhof Café in Berlin' was highly commended in the Gregory O'Donoghue prize 2016.

Other books include: I wanted to bring you Flowers/*ich kann das alles Erklaeren* (drama) – *Fischer Aachen;* One Summer in Ireland (fiction) – *Klett Stuttgart;* Elbe Letters go West/*Briefe von der Elbe –Blaupause;* Michel the Merman, a story for young people based on Hamburg legends (illustrated by Mark Barnes NZ) – BOD Hamburg.

Tiada Tempat di Rawa (translation into Indonesian),

Kiltimagh – Blaupause (translation into German by poet Mirko Bonné).

www.terry-mcdonagh.com